Betweenness

Betweenness

Varun Ravindran

poems

BAOBAB PRESS

First Edition

ISBN-13: 978-1-936097-60-9

Library of Congress Control Number: 2025935420

Baobab Press
316 California Ave, #24
Reno, Nevada 89509
www.baobabpress.com

For my first teacher, Laura Moeller

Table of Contents

•

Sea Variation 2
At Road's End, Lincoln City, Oregon 3

•

Sea Variation 12
A Poem 13
First Morning in Roslin 16
Sea Variation 17
Pillow Talk 18
"Endless the series of things with no name . . ." 19
"Fear was my father . . ." 20
Arabesque 21

•

The Age of Waters 24

•

Two-Part Invention (for One Voice) 46
Arabesque 47
Sea Variation 48
Schubert's Piano Sonata in B-flat 49
Melville at the Customs House 50
"My peace is gone, my heart is heavy . . ." 51
Arabesque 54

•

RE: RE: NO GIMMICK NO DISAPPOINTMENT NO STRINGS ATTACHED NOTHING TO LOSE FIND LOVE PURE PROFITS LOVE FOR PROFIT OIL FOR MONEY!! 56
Schubert's Cello Quintet 64

•

Season/Body 66
Counterpastoral 69
Gerard Manley Hopkins Drafts the Light 72
The New Astronomy 74
Schubert's Moments Musicaux No. 2 81

Fugue 82
Sea Variation 83

•

Everything That Is Not the Case 86
The City Opposite Nineveh 93
A Lattice 97
"La route chante . . ." 100
Sea Variation 103

Notes 105
Acknowledgments 107

Sea Variation

Yet the other was singing, buckling:
o lovely in milks, in wreathes,
lovely in breaths,

the sea shivers like a prayered tongue —
jubilation, o jubilation,
vanishing swiftly,
as the sea dries its laces in the sun

drying the refuse of faces
faces not there faces no longer there
faces there where the sea was where I was

on a bent green bench
holding and pouring
a singing where I was —

At Road's End, Lincoln City, Oregon

The grouped stanzas below are to be read simultaneously by three voices.The first voice reads only the first line of each stanza and proceeds to the first line of the next; the other two voices do likewise for the second and third lines, respectively. "•" indicates silence.

•
•
I started Early—Took my Dog—

That last day I threw the sheets in the dryer and walked
The early gray sea
And visited the Sea—

to the sea. The gray day's glanced sun, skewed by water,
lanced by light. Askew. Coarse. Bare but where crowned in silver
I started Early—Took my Dog—And visited the Sea—

made water look like hauberk, coarse, bare, unwieldy.
And there rippling like a pinch of talc under breath.
•

(5) Barnacle waged marriage to lichen on the waist
•
•

of the rock I sat on and in a pool by my feet,
Ascetic in its solidity, the sea stark
•

a pale ochre starfish en-penché. The pearlscud horizon
against the soft star of my splayed hand—
The Mermaids in the Basement Came out to look at me—

had an aureole against it, broad, pale as blanched
broad as the plains of the hand—
And Frigates—in the Upper Floor Extended

lettuce, veined in shreds, in ridges of curd-dense cloud.
lined like a hand—the sea a hand in my hand
Hempen Hands—presuming Me to be a Mouse—

Long sea, longlooked sea so long looked at, looked at long,
flexing His fingers — one by one by one by one —
Aground — upon the Sands —

turned unreal, solid, a word in the mouth of my eyes,
by one — Bariolage —
•

repeating over and over and over —
•
•

gray sea dull sea stone sea deep sea blown sea steep sea smooth sea old sea
sea dull sea stone sea steel sea deep sea blown sea steep sea smooth sea lulled
•

lulled sea webbed sea-wet sea-steeped sea-blown sea-lulled sea-tilled sea-tolled
old sea lulled sea webbed sea wet sea steeped sea blown sea tilled sea tolled sea
•

sea-cleft sea-full tilling away, tolling away, counting, falling, counting
cleft sea full sea tilled sea tolled sea falling, counting, full, full —
•

away a silence — the Silence —
•
•

So full of meaning as to lack any. Or I
fills my hand — a hand in my hand —
But no Man moved Me — till the Tide went past

was — and this lack of it brought me — back to the Web of it.
and my hand shakes.
my simple Shoe — and past my Apron —

Along shore each succeeding wave deposited,
•
and my Belt—and past my Boddice—too

and arranged in its own shape thousands of infant
My hand shakes, and the ocean takes it.
And made as He would eat me up—as wholly as a Dew

crabs, infant limbs, tattered shells, kelp,
My hand shook; my grandfather held it.
Upon a Dandelion's sleeve—

eggs, bladders, all knitted into a quilt by powdery
My hand shakes, the other takes it.
And then—I started—too—

water in which, under which, large crabs shone silver
Only the hand holds the hand.
•

and squirmed and exposed their soft pale abdomens
•
•

and mounted each other.
•
•

•
Only the hand holds the hand pouring away.
•

Climbing the stairs back to the road, I meet *you*.
•
•

I touch *you*. We go back to the beach. We sit there
I touched *your* hand.
No Man moved Me — Till the Tide went past —

on gnarled driftwood. The wind, an insomniac,
I tell you about my grandfather.
•

wrinkles and wreathes the sea.
A seagull with a Thales-look surveys with us
•

•
the unmade Bed of the sea.
•

•
•
And He — He followed — close behind — I felt His Silver Heel

•
The house was locked when the sun was a wax seal.
Close behind — I felt His Silver Heel

Behind the golf course at Neskowin, behind lines
•
upon my Ancle —

of bog anemones fringing Little Nestucca,
Between a broken rank of firs (one hollowed of
•

opposite the cheese factory at Tillamook closed
a sudden within a Dysentery of light),
I felt his Silver Heel upon my Ancle — close

for redesign, behind Nehalem opposite Rite Aid;
opposite Farmer's Creek Market Place selling bulbs,
behind—

•
jam, daffodils, rockfish; behind Nehalem,
•

driving to the mouth of the Columbia,
and finally, behind the slough in Astoria,
•

a wedge of, nail of, or patch of the Pacific is glimpsed—
dots of, an arc of, or a line of the Pacific was glimpsed,
•

never unmoving—
whole as a dew—
I felt His Silver Heel upon my Ancle—

•
•
Then My Shoes would overflow with Pearl—

its silver heel never unmoving, dented,
his silver hand unmoving, dented—
•

denting the things it touches—
•
Until We met the Solid Town—No One He seemed to Know—

•
•
And bowing—with a Mighty look—At me—The Sea withdrew—

"Do not offer outdoor seating when the tide's high,"
That morning I started early, threw the sheets in
•

hisses our waitress at her colleague. "The water
the dryer, and walked down to the heavy sea.
•

can move right under the table." Then to us,
Askew, longlooked, longfaced, aground upon
•

"Today's special: clams. Tomorrow's special, also clams—
the sands, I walked down to the dewy sea falling
•

surprise! Here's some bread. What can I get you?" Our knees
into sea. "Everybody's lonely," my grandfather
•

touch. The table, vast. Shimmering, a brown duck etches
wrote in a last letter, "There's no meaning." That morning
•

circles around a nodding balize counting away
I watched the deep sea, full sea, old sea falling away,
•

the old creaking sea.
rising, tolling away the old creaking sea.
•

Sea Variation

Streaks of wet pastel, the sea around the bridge,
smudged on, smudged between delaminated glass,
sounds of one hand clapping, the sea of commas—

sea tarnished beneath the cliff—
marbling, fleecing, breathing
jasmine unravelling in a skittish wind.

A Poem

A door, or an idea of one, opened, and my grandfather walked into the room of being. I saw him—no, rather I felt him, with a Gold Flake cigarette between his lips, read over my shoulder. "Why Madras?" he asked, pointing at my poem. "You saw that woman in Kathmandu, didn't you?"

"Yes," I said, "but I remember Madras far better than I do Kathmandu."

"So what?" he said. "It's dishonest. Nothing more than a sluttish trinket."

"I'll tell *you* what's dishonest, what's dishonest is spending the whole day away from home, not telling patti, and returning home drunk at two. And you knew how neurotic she was."

"Another dirty fib for your poems. And besides. Nothing wrong with a drink now and then," my grandfather said, brandishing imperiously (the way he checked at chess, tapping the king with a jesterpiece, making a show of not quite toppling the royal) an ashy burnished dandelion, dispersing it.

"No. There certainly isn't," another voice said, "and it really *is* dishonest, what you're doing." Elizabeth Bishop!!—through the idea of the door into the world. "Poetry just isn't *worth* that much," she said, "let me read to you a letter of—"

"I don't need a lecture," I snapped.

"He has always been willful," my grandfather said, "he gets it from me."

"Oh, but he got the beginning of this poem from *me*," Elizabeth Bishop said, reading over my other shoulder.

"Elizabeth! Did you know they've published all your letters?" I said nastily, "I've read them all."

"Heavens!" said Elizabeth Bishop.

"What are you getting at with this poem anyway?" my grandfather said.

"I essay here, grandfather, nothing less than an inexorable proof of the lack of a Selfhood," I said.

"Oh dear," Elizabeth Bishop said. "But Father Hopkins would have something to say about *that*. Why is he not here, if I may ask?"

"There was never room enough in the world for Father Hopkins," I said.

"When you say 'world,' you mean 'poem,'" sneered my grandfather, "Is that right? Is that how it goes? Am I a poet?"

I ignored him and continued to write, my grandfather and Elizabeth Bishop peering over each of my shoulders—

• • •

—murmuring
beneath the earth,
chirping beneath
the chime, folding,
unfolding, in his palm,
on mine—like music,
we're mapped of time.
Perceptions, for example.
I perceive blue. But the I
that perceives blueness is
not the I that first perceived
blue, or even previously
perceived blue. Rather, this
I recalls all the past I's
that perceived blue: a blur
first, maybe, then a splotch
and a square, then a sky
and a color and a crayon
and a mood and a music.
Mandelstam says every I
is a wallowing boat, all
added up to a bridge by
a future which then crosses
it. Looks across a bruise of a bay.
But I remember the woman selling
peanuts in Madras, singing by
the fractured sea. Seeing our
camera she asked for a picture.
"But where would she hang it,
her hut," an aunt sneered.
A stray white wise dog considered
us from under the cart, his paws
crossed. The woman straightened
her spine, her blue sari, and the jasmine
in her hair. Her red glass bangles slid
down her hand. The moon was a translucent

nail. The sea was a taut cheesecloth patched
all over. The sea was the Bay of Bengal.
The dusk or the sea, dark lilac,
and the waves like lilac hinges
in dark still sand—and I too became
(or am I becoming *now*?) dark and still
and at one with something—
with the sea, with the world, the woman,
whatever—like a shadow.
I felt or feel now unreal, feel now
or felt a surge of joy thinking about the places
my grandfather would take me to,
the Aries Lending Library run by one woman from her apartment
on Third Street, Nehru Nagar, Madras, Chennai, India, the places in the world, the idea of the door closed, my grandfather and Elizabeth Bishop continue not to be. I realized then that I had never told my grandfather that I missed him, that for a long time he was my only friend. I would confess to him, if such things were allowed, that it terrifies me that I am watching my father become, from the decaying lip to the liver, his own father. My grandfather understands the unsaid, the unanswerable, the compromises, and embraces me. I would ask him, if such things were allowed, to cross a puddle, to cross a bridge, a border, how, how many, how many lifetimes?

First Morning in Roslin

The rooster, the bicycle bell, the seagull
tapping loam to lure out worms — even the sea;
none of these unexpected. But then,

offstage, a drunken trombone slurring
wayward melody, a Schubert melody: an engine
pulling his tin-thatch wares around a gorge.

A cow, maybe, lowing up slopes of plush and thistle,
dung, dome, dew. And her bell: a flattened
soup-can, halved and set loose by a Demiurge, around

two clanging pebbles and a rusted key. This light
makes flesh of things; mired in skin the eye
only traces the ripening-outward to soundfell where air

pleats like muslin; air, like music, sound tran-
substantiated, lashing in, out of being, brimming
once more my grandfather, his hand in mine

a sparrow. And a street in Madras ends in a row of huts,
and a woman selling peanuts sings, breaks your heart,
and at the periphery the mackled crescent

of sunthrush sea throbbing as behind a throat.
Enclosed by nothing, attached to nothing,
all-entwined, like rain, it's that sea murmuring

beneath chirps, chimes, beneath silversilt-origami-
light so freely given, folding, unfolding, in his palm,
on mine, the dirt, a word ever on the verge, the sea.

Sea Variation

Lovely as milk, smooth as a knell,
bodiless and made of breaths,
a blue bed of pollen,

lace, mesh, the sea ran
like a prayered tongue, the waves
shining where they fell, so many eyes of needles.

Pillow Talk

for Patrick Walsh

—and it's raining, so I kiss your beard, and—love is something one must—move in—I
think but but how Rilke's blackbird moves, moves in, moves in that space made by the hands,
cleared with his hands—

—and Rilke's rain is a plover, a tapestry—and Goethe's rain flits and flits between—
between what, "dark earth and heaven," wet earth and heaven, and this rain sounds like
an old clock—

—and this rain wound, wound eighteen years ago, and rounding its circuit,
and finding instead of the nose it could've landed on—in a porch in Madras now Chennai
where my grandpa, with his liver like tinned mango, rummaging through an atlas,
his mind, tells me how long the Nile is, the Snake, and other waters and other
waters, and storms on Annapurna, and quiet low roads in Nepal and above, above
them, always before them that great white thumbprint in the sky—a vacancy.

The world is vast.
It is raining, it was raining, it will rain.

And *you*, my Bratsche, who are here.

Your beard is russet, gold, straw, ricelight, a steep deep burring prairie—your
eyes are blue—
your limbs are long—a slightness, breathmark on the forehead, center-left, a boy on
the wet earth from the Tualatin and a dark dog named Dusty, and once you were a boy
away from me—and between us, containing us, this, this enduring, even then this—
This, the only given, wrung from flesh, flung fresh, *This* suffused as breath through reed,
saying nothing more than,

Here is a word, here is the world.
Here song, here breath.
Here. Find yourself now—

—you, you who are here, you, sparrow of my hours, thresh-in-heart,
seabreath pouring through my window, I find you, I step inside you, I love you.

"Endless the series of things with no name . . ."

Ogunquit, 10/28/2016

No willing how no willing   how sandpipers
arranging
songs as if   knowing
all   along knowing   that off-mind
plagal
solving car   horn   how this body
how words   roaming   which   circumferences
till a flare into meaning   how
between   fingers   the frock   light as lash

foil
coming
to itself   only
inside   lusts   and   stings
no willing no willing
how this crushglass allaliveness
pricking
flesh and eye suffused
holding all   at once
unwilled   brine   birds   rains   i
how   seaside
(sea heaps
blown-on   flour)   these two
i's   on open sill this
oboe   how
for this mess of
tones   bartering breathtwine

"Fear was my father . . ."

Next to the toilet, you gave your hand to me.
Your arm was the girth of a cello's neck—
your face an oldmanface, your hand a boy's hand.

Reek of ethanol, piss, corn. You had missed
the bowl. Down among the piss strewn on the floor
you were giving one hand to me.

The other was hugging the damp ceramic. Your robe
kinked around your thigh, exposing
your purple sex. I saw that oldmanface, that boy's hand;

I pulled away. I ran for the nurse who
lifted you, scolded you, wiped you, placed you back in bed.
You had given your hand to me.

You pretended sleep, now meek, now shy, and I glad
you did: ashamed of your old, your old old-
manface, of your boy's hand asking for mine,

I sat braying with gratitude. And I was enough
for neither you nor me when you gave
your hand to me, your face to me, my
oldmanface to me but your little boy's hand—

Arabesque

one gull on the air
    one crow in the fir

        sun in on through the cut rain
            standing between the door

                the sea—
                    whose hinges chirping?

The Age of Waters

for
G. C. Waldrep and Robert Bringhurst

The grouped stanzas below are to be read simultaneously by three voices. The first voice reads only the first line of each stanza and proceeds to the first line of the next; the other two voices do likewise for the second and third lines, respectively. "•" indicates silence.

Water-Music

•
•
In the Age of Waters in Tualatin, Oregon,

•
•
standing water looks out of itself—then, moving

•
•
water. Water heavy, indefatigable,

•
During the Ages of Waters in Oregon,
looks out from the pit of its ice near Missoula,

(5) •
water pulled to light, water with breasts of glaciers,
moves, creeps towards the crumble of the holding

•
skin of silts—water dispersing "contracting into a span"—
continent, carving valleys, making sleeves for the rivers—

Back in the Age of Waters, the Age of Wet
dragged towards the core—seeping, dripping, roaring
but now barred by walls, tarries inland, now—

and Waters, water was dragged and kept in stone pits,
into, on through the stone of the Ages of Waters, nets
now deepening—now, now deepening, deepening, now

but soon burst out—"meandering sluggishly across
of water, mouths of water, scrolls, blots of water, smirches
bursts through Wallula, Umatilla, spans from Walla Walla

valley in braided channels, oxbows, sloughs, sandbars,
of water smirching water—
to Crown Point, drowns Crown Point, builds Alameda,

riffles," moving water, nets of water, wounds of water,
wreathes of water, leaves of water—
carries Montana, Palouse, down, down, down into itself—

churches of water, now blown on by the wind
water condensed—then—
along the Columbiana, mothering lakes,

of the Age of Water—
an exhalation—
lakes, and lakes, scattering argillite, uranic

•
kenosis of water beneath the wind in the wilds,
granite, unites, combines itself, to the water,

•
the wild mindlessnesses of the Ages of Waters
and the water of the ocean of the Age of Waters—

•
in Tualatin, Oregon—in the Ages of Waters
•

blown-on,
in Tualatin, Oregon, wind or, or—breathing,
•

now, now grown-on, grown-on waters of the Age of Wet
in the waters, now, a breathing-in, of the water,
•

and Waters, on whose smear the tip of the fern blossoming long
now in the now of the water of the Ages of Waters,
•

slurs draws a wavering V—aquatic water, amphibian water,
during the waters of the Age of Waters, in Columbiana—
•

“part of it crawling, part of it about to crawl,” wraiths, wraiths of water
•
•

in the frills of gills, and breathed-in water—breathed-on water—
•
•

breathed in, froth of the bond of the broth of the breaths
•
In the Age of Waters, in TUALATIN, OREGON,

and the breaths of the Age of Waters in TUALATIN, OREGON—
                Flowing out of the cave of an age of the Ages
silent water—

•
of Waters, the Ages of Stone stirred to the softness
•

•
of an ear, of a lupin, of water, or of daffodil,
During the Age of Waters in Tualatin, Oregon,

•
talc daffodils, talc faces thronging the waters
unheard water looked out of itself—

•
in the Ages of Waters, water of green — rivers
•

"Green River," WILLAMETTE, river without sides,
of green, green rivers, green river, WILLAMETTE, river
•

moving water moved and moving out of the Age
of green, flowing, dark green —
•

of Stone, Age of Wet and Water, Age of Ice, Age
Green rivers, gold laden —
•

of Spore, Age of Gills and Bellows, Bellowing Water —
rivers of riches — the milks of the salts from the silts
Green rivers, gold-laden, rivers of riches —

•
from the Ages of Water —
the silts and the ashes and the salts from the breasts

— in the Age of Waters in
•
of the Age of Waters — WALL-LAMT, WILARMET, WALLAMETTE,

the COLUMBIANA, standing water looks out —
•
WILLAMETTE, river greened, spilling, gold-laden, where

of itself then — moving water, gold-laden, where seals
During the Ages of Water in TUALATIN
"water ripples and runs fast," green river, gold-laden,

swim under the steeps, the “high walls of basalt with sudden
OREGON — standing water looked of itself —
river of beavers, lampreys, salmon, slaves, seals, canoes

cracks in them” — and the buoyant Siren whose snout made
•
hollowed in thick fire, rivers of tongues, tongues of rivers,

the snorting of tame horses in the water, whose fat
•
CHINOOK, KALAPUYA, TUALATIN, YONCALLA; rivers

competed with the “best Holland butter” and reeked
•
of riches, rivers of teeth, rivers of beads, meats,

and reeked of fresh fresh almonds; “placid, loyal,
•
abalone brought up from the GREAT BASIN, down

loving, and delicious,” snuffling right up to the boat’s
•
from WALLA WALLA, UMATILLA; rivers of frogs,

wallowing gunwales, “first one foot, then the other, as cattle
During the Ages of Waters in TUALATIN —
rivers of Frog Women, Coyote; free, undammed waters —

do, sheep do, when they graze, and thus with a gentle motion
OREGON — standing water looked out of itself — then, moving
In the age of the green river, gold-laden green rivers,

half-swim, half-walk” half in the shining, soiling, clanging,
waters, green, gold-paved, commodious commodity
winding through fires, rivers of sextants, of schooners,

diaphene—   half on a dogged blade
of waters pawing and pawing the waterwheels,
of gunpowder, of beavers and otters bashed with boulders

too blunt for blubber—and the otters, “stupid, sluggish,
green rivers, gold-laden, aboriginal green scooped, drunk,
and bartered with the Russians, the Spaniards, the British

surly, sleepy, forever sleepy, capturable
tippling musical through the windows, plucked waters,
stumbling upon and naming Cape Foulweather, Perpetua—

without any painstaking, any ingenuity,”
slurs of water bowed out the cave of the age of the Ages
rivers of riches, rivers of Good-and-Bounty, rivers

frantic, strangling in the nets knotting around loose
of Water in Tualatin, Oregon, when standing
of commerce and plenty and schooners filled with otter skins,

eyes, chewing off their own forepaws—
water looked out of itself, moving, water
beaver skins, bound for Macau, the Pearl River,

800 otters in the holds of tiny St. Peter—
indefatigable, mothering itself,
Whampoa—pelts of creatures from and of the waters

and the mush, those sea-cows at last obstinate,
its own great- great- grandkin—
from the Age of Waters, sold for tea, silks,

sticking to barrels, to wood teeth; 800 otter pelts
green rivers, gold-laden, waters of slurs and insects,
cinnamon, desks, and cups and saucers splashed with arabesques

sewn onto coats in CHINA with sandalwood buttons—
diseased water, heavy, dropsical with breath and disease
of blue cranes, blue water, blue forests—rivers of riches,

WILLAMETTE, green river, gold-laden, "river of sickness"—
rivers of argosies returning from the faraways,

malarial river, variolal river of the settler's headcold—
bustling like Batavia and bearing "alter-pieces

WILLAMETTE of treaties and disease; WILLAMETTE,
reworked in Asia with gold and silver" given by LIMA,

SALMON, LITTLE and BIG NESTUCCA, stocked with fish, rivers
POTOSI, NUEVA GRANADA—abundance, abundance—

of game and hunt, rivers of abundance, of giving,
abounding waters, generous, waters

rivers of giving, given rivers of giving, rivers
of generosity, generous waters of the ROGUE,

of taken-away waters, rivers of taking, gold-laden,
the DESCHUTES, the TILLAMOOK, MACKENZIE, taking, o gladly

green, WILLAMETTE, SALMON, YAMHILL halving the given land,
taking tattered leather, a broken bayonet, tipsy

•
land made under the waters of the Ages of Waters,
kettles, two chipped bronze USA buttons; yielding coats,

•
land of horses, land of tangled tongues—UPPER UMPQUAS,
hats, gloves, tapestries, curtains; always returning, accruing,

•
TAKLEMA, KALAPUYA, CHINOOK WAWA,
green rivers, green abundance, abundance of green,

•
YONCALLA, ENGLISH; given land of the "language-houses," horses,
ASTORIA, CHAMPOEG, FORT WILLIAM gleaming green in the green

In the Age of Wet and Water in TUALATIN, OREGON,
horse races, treaties-then-assurances to the 400 left—
waters of the GREAT RIVER OF THE WEST, fertile seal-bearing

standing water looked out of itself—then, moving water—
            400 left to the ceded waters made
beaver-breeding otter-giving waters, waters up which,

•
in the Ages of Water in Tualatin, Oregon, when standing
        into a hundred, a thousand, a million ripplings of havocs

•
water looked: moving waters—
of greens, a breathless otter stumbles, chokes, pursued by stones,

•
•
pursued by nets, by bayonets, a faulty bayonet—

A Santiam Story

One day Coyote was going along the water, going along towards the falls.
When dark fell, he made camp.
When light fell, he went on.
Then dark again—he made camp.
Then light—again he was going along.
Dark—he made camp.
Light—Coyote was going along.
Dark—he made camp in a sweathouse.
There Coyote sucked his own cock.

"This news will not escape," Coyote said,

"This sweathouse will be a rock."

And he turned the sweathouse into a rock.
Then Coyote was going along.
Coyote was going along the green river,
when he saw a canoe with people in it singing songs.
Coyote said,

"What's the news?"

No one answered.
He became afraid and said:

"What's the story? What's the story?"

Someone in the canoe said,

"What in the world? Oh, it's that Coyote! Hello!"

"Hello! What's the news?"

"Oh, no news at all, no story at all," someone said, "the only new thing is that Coyote was sucking his penis."

Then water carried the canoe along.
Coyote was surprised:

"But who saw me? Where was he standing, I wonder? I will go back to the sweathouse and see where he was standing."

Coyote was going along. He reached the sweathouse and studied it.
Coyote saw that the rock had a tear all down its side.

"I see," Coyote said,

"Then this is where the story came out from. Everything will know what I did. Then this is how it's going to be, and how it will always be. Everything will know the secrets. Nothing will ever be completely hidden: that is how it will always be—

WATER-MUSIC

•
During the Ages of Waters in TUALATIN, OREGON—
In the Age of Waters in OREGON,

During the Age of Waters in TUALATIN, OREGON—
given lands, lien lands, titled lands of lines and fences,
froth of the bond, bond of the breath, bond of the froth of the breath,

•
senators, land of laws, “laws of land” ratified,
when standing water looked out of itself—then, moving water—

froth of the bond, broth of the breath, bond of the froth of the breath,
and ratified so “they shall again receive the same
•

(5) “degged with dew” the ages, and Ages of Water looked—
punishment until they shall quit the country—”
•

standing OREGON, TUALATIN in Waters of Age, waters
ceded lands of laws, bylaws, titles, deeds, states, steeples,
“degged with dew, dappled with dew, the groins” of the ages

of ague, waters of algae, yellowlegs, flu, flutes—
wires, justice—green-shouldered, nail-bright COLUMBIA
the water threads through and looks out of itself—water,

lupins, daisies, and orphan cottonwood roots, chinooks, chubs,
brought down from the Ages of Gills and Waters—degged with age,
water of silence, or water of sounds unheard, looked

cutthroat trout, egrets, fish ladders, herons, ruffed grouse,
dappled with age, the land spurted out the breast of deep deep
out itself—then—then itself out, looked unheard—sounds of water,

macropthalmic lampreys, belled arbutus ripening
waters from the Age of Waters in COLUMBIANA
or silence of water moving—looked, water, standing—

in the rocks—the WILLAMETTE FALLS PAPER COMPANY,
when standing water looked out itself—then—itself out,
MISSOULA, BONNEVILLE, in Waters of Age—

in the roar near Skookum's buried tongue, the locks,
the looked water, COLUMBIANA, standing in waters of age,
•

given land sold back to federated GRAND RONDE—
in SILETZ, in GRANDE RONDE—
WILLAMETTE, river of green, gold-laden, "place where water

WILLAMETTE, green river, gold, laden, looked—
•
"ripples and runs fast," making and unmaking from the Age

water, standing in waters of age, Crone WILLAMETTE,
WILLAMETTE—
of Waters, fresh WILLAMETTE, fallow, fallow waters—

made and unmade—
breathed-in, breathed-on—ashy place where the water
•

Willamette, crone river all out of the Age of Waters, made
ripples and runs fast, looked out of itself—crowned in firs
•

and unmade, like the wind blowing through all the ages,
and fire, running down hillocks from which the KALAPUYA
•

all the ages of the Age of Waters—
looked out, year after year, at their fire, burning away all
Fallow waters, fallow,

•
the undergrowth, making new the savannah-face—
fallow as a gap or cave or hole or hollow, a valley

WILLAMETTE, pooling and standing in the waters
WILLAMETTE, old WILLAMETTE growing, and growing,
and hollow— WILLAMETTE, WHILAMUT, tongue-barren

of age,—making, unmaking, looking, unlooking—
and growing younger and younger in the Ages of Waters
WALLAMT, making, unmaking from the Age of Waters,

a moccasin flaking its makings—
growing older, crone WILLAMETTE, growing—
looking, unlooking, flaking its makings as tongues, gods,

•
WILLAMETTE, growing, flaking its makings—
winds—out of itself, braiding and banking in TUALATIN,

•
•
Oregon, which only accumulates—

The Zodiac of Midges

Palace of waters,
of green dark silence,
the dark green profound

sired of water
rubbing water
place of water
stone, mountains,
place of firs, sheer

green as dusk, place
of dusk. Place of dusk
like rain. Place of rain.
Place of rain

like consciousness
abyss, plenum
sea-palace

place of seas
valleys shine-creased,
lupin-creased

porousness
a pouring,
a pouringplace
into which sound—

and *me*—

into all of it—
teeth strung along neat rains

tossed in the breast-

soft dark all night—

the sounds of water—

wet and bit the black rocks

• • •

Mt. Hood
Hood River
Grace Su's China Gorge
"41 years in the same place"

stranded humpbacks

the water, the soil, the soil,

soil beneath, beneath all of it
aged, ageless, siletzia
thrusting out here, there
into the dewy light,
adopted, named Crescent
and Roseburg—
wet, dark, moss-bit
ancient, ancestral, dark
rock, wet-dark stone,
high up the family tree,
dark rose blossoming
dark, darkly, in dark—

to *be*—
to be *poured*—
into all this—

beinghoods—
a beingness—

discovered?
Built? If built,
I always touch
the things I know,
if discovered
I know only
the things I touch—

which is it—
what is it—
touches now,
now the hem

of this vapory
midday matter

the "firm water,
cold flame,"
the enmackerelled PACIFIC—

—being
being poured

dumb, dumb,
into dark—

dark silence
beneath the green

places of—
palace of—
COLUMBIANA!—

raining, the rain
(wet dark)
place of—rain—
ceaseless—still—
dark, dark
waterfalls—
tumult—of waters—but—
"but how shall I . . .
make me a room . . .
reach me . . ."

• • •

{ *water, endless rain*
the sound
.

{ *the water's sinews,*
of the flowing mountains,
rain, endless water

{ *the folded stones —*
of lent-out bones — water
mountains flowing

{ .
.
in the sound —

"In another part of the field . . ."

. . . and where the James rises, the sun is a gorged capitalist,
the field battered-out gold, the brindled cows rising,
lowering, their dumb heads per the epicycles of the swarm
around — but my father, dad, appa, whatever it is you should
call your sire, seed, gateway (gate in? out?) — mummy-like
in the backseat. Once because he lay delirious, I watched
the dying dog at my f——'s House — I opened drawer after
drawer to catalog a world. Scraps of blank paper (what for?),
bills, blue BIC pens, staples, Lifesavers, Bowmore —
Milky Ways, keys to those older houses we lived in, jellybeans,
Q-Tips — I thought: my unasked-for f—— with a sweet tooth
would have eaten chocolate today. And my poor Maddy in pain.
I laid next her on her bed. She panted all night in my ear.

Virginia is all edge and mist and halfglow and shadow,
and mountains which "are the soul of the Region,"
a pamphlet assures me. "How do the mountains, the minerals

of which the rocks are made, affect the people of the mountains?"
Since an Age of Waters, "some deltas have grown, some volcanoes
have erupted. The mountains and rivers appear much the same."

"Have fun," my f——— says, and a nurse ushers him inside.
My f——— holds a small suitcase holding a month of clothes.
He carries a backpack and an iPod filled with songs. My f———
holds his back very straight. His head still holds forth high.
His head where scotch displaces all the songs when he dives
the bottles. My balding f——— walks with a straight spine.

The mountains are moving — because we are driving.
"They rise out of the sea, you see," my pamphlet says,
which I've grown to love during. This pamphlet shall be
my f———!!! "They rise out of the sea, you see," my father
says, "and wear down to roots" — birthing OREGONS, VIRGINIAS —
heron-women, waterstriders — and my balding father played
tennis once, and bit his nails down to crescents —

but what a laugh it is, what terror, to be born, and to be in a car,
to fuck, to beget, to propagate, to to where, where "plutons are
scattered," whatever that means, where something and other
things are always happening, and some other things are
happening also, things I can't see, I can't see in this OLD DOMINION,
this VIRGINIA COUNTRY deep deep deep night dark enough to stain
teeth, Sirius bright enough to itch them — "Look," he said once
at an airport, "that rain — under the lamp — it looks like strings."

My balding father, I will say one day, walked with a straight
spine. My father, I will say one day to Durga and Miranda
(dogs? daughters?) swelled, turned, fruited like a lotus

in the music, the way *I* do — speaking of — sit, sit, *sit*!
I shall now play my viola for you, now listen close —

• • •

In the backseat, a HIMALAYA feeling—cold, rocky, high, bright,
pure, blue, free, alone, free. Rummaging through the rocks of oneself—
leftover after the collision of plates or shelves or somesuch (o my
laminated father long lost in the crease of the cushion!)—I am
now free, I said to myself, and so I may as well make a list of things
to think about for the rest of my life. Yes, let's see—sahajiyas, VAN
DUZER trees, and time, and people I desperately want to sleep with—
Anton Chekhov definitely—and movement, and music, which
is movement after all—born in Madras, flew over the never-resting
seas to this backseat—BACKSEAT—in VIRGINIA, and now in WEST VIRGINIA,
but never EAST VIRGINIA, no, never. And I add "Names" to this list.
And "The Mind." The full mind, the free mind, the mind soaring
like a mountain, the "mountainous mind" free, free, free, free, and, but—

—but *what's* free? What's freedom? Do you get it, earn it?
Be of it, become in it? Is it a state? And, or, of, being, doing?
Statelessness? An estate?

But where's the meaning in all this sudden nonsense?
Where? Where has everything gone? Where are they going?
What is it that hides the meanings? What is it that grinds them down?
What grinds down the mountains?
What grinds down the father? Himself? His own father? His boy?
His boy? What grinds him down, the father, despite the love?
Despite the love, what grinds down the father?
What, despite, what, what grinds down the, the love?
A boy? What is it that grinds down? Despite the love
what grinds down a love? What grinds down what grinds? What?

what is — nowhere

to go to — nowhere

to go — nothing

to know — no one to be —

the borrowed place —

nevernamed borrowed place —

always the borrowed

place — like a language

prefigured by the basins

it plays in — but within

its confines absolute —

absolute — absolutely,

Two-Part Invention (for One Voice)

Music: Time that one wants neither
to arrest nor hasten.
—*Simone Weil*

Running from. Running to. Running whence for who where to.

Now girdling. Now girdled. Now what is is. Is mindwide.

What is is. And is windlong, wide as a mind, sea-height.

Seahigh now now poised on a reef. On a pin. Pinned

to a pricking asking.

Running from or to and from where?

For who?

To? To who? You?

You or me? Me? Running to me?

From now?

Me or you now soft as a steamed envelope, hushed as fading coal?

Me or you now perched on a cage swung from a long, wrung, tow?

What can be is—

But what is, me or you, and where to?

What is is—

And where? In what fading like hushed coal

What can be is now— *hushed like the stone in*

the wet rut of a rush

O what is is now, *of a ripening plum?*

is now swinging on a long, wrung, tow—

Arabesque

for Lhasa de Sela, who is also the speaker

Xochipilli, I won't insist on more than this,
this ajar thing called "Lhasa," in the morning
more than this breath, making and falling

into morning. Given what we're given.
Skin, tongue. Skin to tongue. Thigh to fold,
breeze. Breeze like scouring hands or hours
breeze full of hours the hour we fondle—

Xochipilli, I won't insist on more than this:
this river in an ajar morning both hearse, cradle,
unbraiding, extending, holding, forgetting.

Sea Variation

The sea was drying its laces
in the sun. The bored wind
nosed one corner of translucent

paper. From the pier, three
lines went down into the brassy
sea which shone in belted buckles.

Schubert's Piano Sonata in B-flat

11/17/2017

For 30 years the blue-boaed flame perched
          on kindling has done its striptease
halting, awkward—but this November morning
erect as though enclosed, watching rivers,
          their furrows, steeples, potholes, all
of Pittsburgh catch, hitch in the trawl of, of
morning, the glow of a finger held to flame,
          and singing, "my hands and heart are tied,
but I'm scared of almost nothing at all—"

30 years!

          Schubert who died the November of 1828
chirrups. In its third movement the first theme
          returns breathless, a swallow on the lintel,
          amassing mud, twine, hair, to replace lint by lint
its nest crumbling more, more, the fallen
          the falling stuff, neither replaceable; breathless,
          not uncheerful, roused inside a sudden
measure where fire finds grooves in the blown
          breath, climbs them, and volition is imperative—

Melville at the Customs House

The sea's face wavers
between crone and virgin—
speckle, spangle, powder,
scroll, spindle, spine, prism,
scale, husk, altar, dandelion-
dragonings, skeinspring

all-dwindle, lord, the sea
lord the sea your seeing
the bight gathers, gathers
its lashings and glasses.
Wind your hearing holds,
primes, to your bourdon.

Tuft, beak, this blur your fondle,
flushes, flexes, feels, is—
I sing me—only I sing—
only me. Groan, me, pustule,
molder, me, me, I bound
with, between things,
dandering long in this pit
of tendon, wringing words from

sparrow, bow, o my jade
tremolo, trill touching farthest
shores, we are overtone—

"My peace is gone, my heart is heavy . . ."

Transcription of Schubert's "Gretchen am Spinnrade"

. . . gone, gone, muslins bartered for moths, gone,
gone as far to me, as far as Egypt, gold, calico, as far his
brass, fustian, his boot's rosettes, his ankles

I'm thrown between, on a wheel, spancelled, his wet hands, my neck,
cupping, building, loosening, lengthening, the hole in me,
his hands clenching far away as far from me as me, far where—

wherever he is not there I am not also

Where he is not, my mind—my silk, my subject—

Gone where—where is my—my mind—where—

Where my mind is not is not where my mind is not—

Where my mind is not, there, here—

Where he is not the light dresses without the pierce
without the dwelling this floor, this roof, even far Egypt,
even this dimity and mother-of-all this shame

the shameless cracked open sods of the Ephesians even,

I am a grave where, when he is not inside,

gone, gone—gone as muslins at the market, as silks at the damp—

Inside I keep for him, I glance out for only him, but thresholds trumpet

In all the rush of him water dams for him threshes for him

• • •

The woof and the warp and all the loom for him—

Proves his law the daisy shucked for him

And the shuttle—the shuttle of his shut-in heart breeds the wind I glut in

The words gang in the gong of my thought of his thought, my hands fumble towards, towards,—

My hands!—My hand branches on the wheel—
glints like flies' wings—blossoms on the wheel—
falls to the wheel—my hand climbs—crawls—skirts my hand to be—

to be my hand—to flick this reel—to be ringed
In this, this amethyst, to be my My—but—could—him—
slowly him—who would touch—me touching, him touching

His pharaoh's walk in rippling flax displacing the Me always

In all the elms and cockerels—to make a dog of, to *poodle* me

His wet breath's lines, sugar my mouth takes, smelts, reels to drag me to his ropes and god

His crumpling temple chest will crumple forever and ever and ever and ever

His mouth, his lip's word-to-life alchemy high and closed, rim to his Crownlands—of him, his thronging

An exiling his breath—but my mother—his tongue and his mouth his

Avarice like avarice of the wet—I pour my neck loose my hair to wash his bare—

bared—ankles but the—the, mother, his his

• • •

gambroon and—
the bathhouse smell of silted
petticoats
suet-warm
insides to out
out—out in but—the wax my
suet his
his kiss—

—Gone, gone, all gone, gone, gone all of, the way of, laced of—gone. Gone.

Scored for his bellows, strange, calico, strange, strangeness
a strangeness my mind, the mind but his lawless exclave
I wander and wander around in—

to pant, to drink, to swell, a midge in the frothed pool

with its daylong fiat of bread and, and being, to pant

(Kyrie, Kyrie!, down the windows, all through the deep street) to drink

to fill, to swell in the pond of his hands to scatter
to beg to split to milk to soil to squeeze to push to shit

to beg to be to be battered among all his breaths to perish—

a groan on the bridge a throb on the touch a smear on the calf

perish as the sobbing on a string sobbing

gone gone gone gone my peace gone
my heart gone, my peace gone
my heart gone my peace gone—

Arabesque

All I am is
all I'm not.
What can you do?

All I love I
turn to song.
What can you do?

Okay, say I stop singing—
silence turns
into song,
against music
you're always in
the wrong.

If I love I sing. If I
don't I sing.
If I sing I love. If I
don't I sing—

All I am is
all I'm not.
What can you do?

All I love I
turn to song.
What can you do?

Re: RE: NO GIMMICK NO DISAPPOINTMENT NO STRINGS ATTACHED NOTHING TO LOSE FIND LOVE PURE PROFITS LOVE FOR PROFIT OIL FOR MONEY!!

My dear!!

I sit beside a brindled cow.

How are you!

I'm in dire straits.

A perithalasson is the point in the track closest to the sea, and I'm in dire straits because every day my kingdom accrues.

I'm a prince, and I'm in dire straits because every day I accrue.

Dear, I do not want to be lonely in my kingdom.

I no longer want a kingdom. And I do not want to be like this fly here, in this train compartment, dying next to this exorbitant orange, and so I ask you. Please rescue me. Please rescue me and my orange.

Now the train is above a gully and I can feel the sea beyond the strung cities, beyond the immovable Nation-State.

An epithalasson is the point in the track farthest from the sea.

The compartment behind me is filled
with unsecured dulcimers (I am stowed
away on a freight train, I flee my kingdom,
I sit beside a bridled cow).
When the train jerks I hear these notes:

Then I imagine I hear each's array of oversounds,
and I think: the soul, too, is an argosy—
an argosy of—

Could it be?! Ah, the world! Oh, the world! Yes, yes! It is a junco I hear in the next compartment, among all the dulcimers! It is the bird pecking the dulcimer's radicles!! I pet the cow, I watch the sea. I listen to the bird, the radio, the song on the radio, I am inspired, I write a sonnet, I stop, I think "But why write a sonnet?" I think "But why make things say *Why? Why? Why? Why?*" I shall write a sonnet, I write a sonnet.

O, baby, baby enkindler of my furnace
Heart, how dark the world has now become!
The self once bathed in the sea's plangent dun
Has turned deaf: all harmony, now wrongness.
Viscous, sour, it's regret that floods my tongue
Which, stunned in its set orbit, can't digress:

"I shouldn't have, shouldn't have let him go,
He was, was here, now he's out of sight . . ."— o
I am slave to tongue—tongue slave to mind who
Prays to No-God that he still believes, still believes.
Loneliness kills. Worlds pass me—I'm a sieve
That holds only you, your kind—but all's your kind—
My flame, my wind, my wick, my match, fan me, reeve,
Entwine in me my light, my flint, strike me one more time!

The shadow of the moving bird has its home somewhere indoors. The moving bird inside a box itself moving. But, tell me, are the dulcimers moving, and in relation to who to what to when to where to why? "By which I mean," (as the poets say),

§A Check only **one** of the following three boxes. Is the soul (the soul here being equivalent to the referent of any of the following as found in Form D-959 (a) (iv): beinghood, being, selfhood, self, mind, brain, inscape, ego, atman, brahma, psyche, deferent, eccentric, punctum equans, kokoro, The Here and Now, character, ethic, habit, time, intellect, perception, qualia, brain states a-k, brain states l-o, brain state p, brain state q, brain state p or q, brain states p-v, brain states s-u, brain state v, brain state w, brain state v or w, brain state v simultaneous with brain state w, brain state v and w, brain states x-z, brain states a-z excluding brain state v, consciousness. Append the corresponding proof and/or evidence to form D-959 (A) (I) (iv) and submit along with the entirety of Form D-959),

(a) □« The train?

(b) »□ The dulcimer?

(c) □« ?

§B Check only **one** of the following thirteen boxes **only** if (a) or (b) was selected in **§A** and no proof and/or evidence was submitted. Is the soul (the soul here being equivalent to the referent of any of the following as found in Form D-959 (a) (iv): beinghood, being, selfhood, self, mind, brain, inscape, ego, atman, brahma, psyche, deferent, eccentric, punctum equans, kokoro, The Here and Now, character, ethic, habit, time, intellect, qualia, brain states a-k, brain states l-o, brain state p, brain state q, brain state p or q, brain states p-v, brain states s-u, brain state v, brain state w, brain state v or w, brain state v simultaneous with brain state w, brain state v and w, brain states x-z, brain states a-z excluding brain state v, consciousness. Append the corresponding proof and/or evidence to form D-959 (A) (I) (iv) and submit along with the entirety of Form D-959),

(d) »□ The silent dulcimer?

(e) □« The bird-touched dulcimer?

(f) »□ The palsied dulcimer?

(g) □« The muted dulcimer?

(h) »□ The raining dulcimer?

(i) □« The strings of the dulcimer?

(j) »□ The hammers of the dulcimer?

(k) □« The sounds (but not music) from the dulcimer?

(l) »□ The music (but not sounds) from the dulcimer?

(m) □« The sounds (including music)from the dulcimer?

(n) »□ The oversounds of the sounds (including music) from the dulcimer?

(o) ◻« The sounds (including music) and oversounds from the dulcimer taken together?

(p) »◻ ?

§C Check only **one** of the following two boxes **only** if (c) was selected in **§A** **and** (p) was selected in **§B**. Is the soul (the soul here being equivalent to the referent of any of the following as found in Form D-959 (a) (iv): beinghood, being, selfhood, self, mind, brain, inscape, ego, atman, brahma, psyche, deferent, eccentric, punctum equans, kokoro, The Here and Now, character, ethic, habit, time, intellect, perception, qualia, brain states a-k, brain states l-o, brain state p, brain state q, brain state p or q, brain states p-v, brain states s-u, brain state v, brain state w, brain state v or w, brain state v simultaneous with brain state w, brain state v and w, brain states x-z, brain states a-z excluding brain state v, consciousness. Append the corresponding proof and/or evidence to form D-959 (A) (I) (iv) and submit along with the entirety of Form D-959),

(q) ◻« All of the above?

(r) »◻ In *you*, reader—must it be to be read by you?

If and only if (r) is checked, check **all that apply**, and append the corresponding proof and/or evidence to form D-959 (A) (I) (iv) and submit along with the entirety of Form D-959. What is being read by you?

(i) ◻« Beinghood
(ii) »◻ Being
(iii) ◻« Selfhood
(iv) »◻ Self
(v) ◻« Mind
(vi) »◻ Brain
(vii) ◻« Inscape
(viii) »◻ Ego
(ix) ◻« Atman
(x) »◻ Brahma
(xi) ◻« Psyche
(xii) »◻ Deferent

(xiii) □« Eccentric
(xiv) »□ Punctum equans
(xv) □« Kokoro
(xvi) »□ The Here and Now
(xvii) □« Character
(xviii) »□ Ethic
(xix) □« Habit
(xx) »□ Time
(xxi) □« Intellect
(xxii) »□ Perception
(xxiii) □« Qualia
(xxiv) »□ brain states a-k
(xxv) □« brain states l-o
(xxvi) »□ brain state p
(xxvii) □« brain state q
(xxviii) »□ brain state p or q
(xxix) □« brain states p-v
(xxx) »□ brain states s-u
(xxxi) □« brain state v
(xxxii) »□ brain state w
(xxxiii) □« brain state v or w
(xxxiv) »□ brain state v simultaneous with brain state w
(xxxv) □« brain state v and w
(xxxvi) »□ brain states x-z
(xxxvii) □« brain states a-z excluding brain state v
(xxxviii) »□ consciousness

(s) □ « ?

§D Check the following box **only** if (c) was selected in **§A** **and** (p) was selected in **§B** **and** (s) was selected in **§C**. Is the soul (the soul here being equivalent to the referent of any of the following as found in Form D-959 (a) (v): non-beinghood, non-being, non-selfhood, non-self, non-mind, non-brain, non-inscape, non-ego, anatman, abrahma, non-psyche, epicycle upon epicycle, the Still Center, unconsciousness, nonconsciousness, nonconsciousness of any brain state. No proof is required for **§D**),

(t) □ « None of the above?

Soul or not, but the killing sun on the sea's threshing floor.

The sea and the guilt blooms ever larger around the insect
beginning to drown in the irradicable ecstasy of things.

The sea, the sun-striated stridulating sea, the samsara sea, the chirping parrot sea perched on our cage.

Cage? Yes, our cage! The cage, the cage my love, the cage!
The cage is the irradicable ecstasy of things,
things spooked to stillness amidst their irradicable ecstasy:
that Ohio Honey-Hunter, for example (whose life
was chronicled recently by one of my close friends).
Or the Americans, signing petitions condemning the government to mail to the government; the smoke-drunk Americans whispering "so . . . so . . . so . . . so . . ." to their bloodshot government.

To flies in the moving train one mile is a few, some several lightyears.

The obstinate millionaires splendid in oils, in oils, building palaces in high places, shouting, "VOTE! VOTE! VOTE, and forgive yourself!" Ballots and bluster, ballots and bluster!! The array of all the long-armed Gutenbergs echo: "VOTE! VOTE! VOTE and you get to keep what you have but only if you vote for what you have! How wonderful to have! It is never an option to not have, don't even *think* about it, Mister!!"

"Forgive us! Forgive us! Forgive us for being joyous! Forgive us!" sing the poets joyously.

"Yes, exactly! Exactly! Forgive us, one shouldn't be joyous," sing the joyous, obstinate smoke-drunk masses to the obstinately rising sea, "we want to be forgiven: hence, we are kind, we are good! Won't you, won't someone forgive us?"

Perithalasses!!!!! To love and to be dying, o o o the farrago of the soul! To love and to be drowning O, the irradiated farrago of the world!

• • •

The irradicable ecstasy of things.

The irradicable ecstasy of things, the irradicable obstinacy of things.

Yet the obstinate soul does indeed move (**§A**) provided you let it move provided you clear room for it to move in. Yes yes the soul is not a room not a point the soul doesn't assume a point but maybe the soul points.

Yes, the soul does indeed flow to be.
I flee my kingdom.
You flee your kingdom.
He or she or they flee his or her or their kingdom.
We all flee our kingdoms.
Let's give ourselves ourselves.
Datta, Dayadhvam, Damvata,
Shantih, Shantih, Shantih, O

let's let the sea make anarchists of us all ("Vote! Vote! Vote! Vote! Vote," scream those lords in the land, those soil-storers lining their pockets with soil, planning the next state in the stars, "Vote! Vote! Vote! O my children vote, vote and forgive yourself, but more importantly, be forgiven by us, yes, you are worthy!").

Dare we eat the peach?

Yes.

The day will come when a single original orange shall be pregnant with revolution.

Let us turn and overturn. Let us listen to this argosy of blue dulcimers. Let us give ourselves ourselves. Let us give ourselves ourselves. Let us be free, let us be lonely, let us look for our kingdoms in the fleeing, the freedom, for each of our kingdoms flees and drowns day by day. Let us choose our tethers.

To flies in the drowning train one mile is a few some several lightyears.

• • •

Shantih, shantih, shantih, oh my dear!!!!! And so I write to you, my dauphin, my peace, my tether, from the train, the freedom, the kingdom.

It is **EXTREMELY TIME-SENSITIVE**, to be opened **IMMEDIATELY:** let's give ourselves ourselves, nothing but, that fruit each one of us has tasted with ecstasies of stealth.

I love within the place of rising waters—
because of the irradicable obstinacy of things—
see, see, see, love is on me—
I am loving you and I
will love you over
and over, and over
and over I shall easter
you with time and polyphony.

I eat the streaked leaf and bloom you.

Datta, dayadhvam, damvata, hold out both of your fanned hands, my pharaoh:

Here! My tears.

Here! My orange.

I am yours.

Best,

The Prince of Neerkavitha

Schubert's Cello Quintet

In a splinter
between the earth, the brain
the cello, the viola made of hours,
saying—

> it must be, it must be, it must be o
> it must be, it must be, must it be, o must it be
> it must be it must be o it must be . . .

The man with the viola is delving wood.
He's drawing voice from it.

And the man I am must be weeping—
and the boy I was, wading—and across
the music my grandfather—and his long
hands aloft aloft—and the tongue of earth
drags across the mouth of ash
between earth—long in long harp hands—

Season/Body

Line in palm with broad bend, the way mouth wends to swollens counterside or
shuns — the wilder-
nesses — nests of the
pits, each maned, each
shoaled nipple.
Unrolling it, thew clings lip; saltwhetheavy the cock breaching lip — its sounding its
dead reckoning its
savaging of the swal-
lowplace where sound
rises, or word or music
or does not —
when the mould of breath paste of spit made architecture of pubic tangle, in the
deepwarm of
betweenthighs
I — too — Or-
pheus — Phenomen-
ist — looked —
his head aground on its decaying pleasure, the window behind him. His cock his cock
fuck the whole wet
stress of it. The gleam
of it among all the
dull snarl and span-
gle of my glutton's
slaver. Each pulse in
it consequent to each
breath's heft lengthen-
ing drops of seed into
stream.
I pulled, rolled his balls to turn his tongue, tongued thighs ajarer lifted legs delved
damask, rung out in
the goldmesh dusk of
him the cornsilk fold

and pinch of him, the
weight of him the All
of him — eyelash of
tracery, sinew, musk-
shine, chalice, sphincter,
contortion of limb into
limb into limb into
limb into beinghoods
mine, notmine, I all
hole he matter, he ca-
thedral I his volume.
Out the window the doubling time — gleaming looming looming phyllomanic world.
Spring. Finchdregs
flinging through arches
in shaking branches
into the scalloping
eye chokebright sibyl
reading —
"Leaving and leaving all the loams too lurch, pushing off the harbors of rooted feet
feather root but then
turns and returns to
each transfigured
freckle — returns
each nest, arbor, each
darkeyed junco muddy
or mudcolor — each
bobolink like bargello
on the birches even as I
rake in my half-
life — my breath in
him-in-me perched
on *me* — tongue in
taint — cock leaking
into a tract of sound
fuck fuck fuck fuck
fuck fuck fuck fuck fuck

sore-eyed sorekneed
a calfchoking in each
hand
"—but if I quaked he would shatter so he quakes sobful of sallow open wing takes
throatful of forest open
mouth claims dewful-
ness dewfulness fullness
which now, now,
"will dissemble and the lissome Huma whose touch-of-shade puts kings in things
never alights—peri-
patetic as music or
knowledge or love or
rain—or the quantum
of a time—

Counterpastoral

The arrangement below is to be read out simultaneously by two voices. The first voice reads text in the first column, as the second voice reads the text in the second column. Once a voice has finished reading its column, it goes to the beginning of the opposite one and repeats the same process. The voices are free to harmonize and/or keep time in their own ways, or not.

1st

Place one is in. Time one is in. Specificities of landscape: flora (flowering), fauna (winged, "wild"), water ("chirping" or "worrying"), wind ("fondling"), light ("tonguing", "swelling", "licking"). Specificities of body: tarsi, patella, sex, ribs, sternum and of course the notch there.

Tongue ("psalming"), throat, throats in the light ("slow, waning"). Wind in the throat, wind of the throat.

Volta:

wind in the throat, wind in the mind.

Memory, language. Language of memory. Aloneness. Aloneness of language.

Aloneness of memory. Loneliness. Loneliness, language, ineffability. But the self the subject but the rapt acre—

2nd

Lily, lily, laurel, lily, finch, crow, swallow, kite in the hollow, sallow, birch, arch, larch, lark, water, light, wind—swollen lilies in a line in light like ichor, light beneath them, light veining them, and light on trunks with barks like glaciers; old, old, old light walking, walking how many miles in its day to water, to the laurel, to the lilies, to a lily,
to the line?

Is it that a field enclosed in a line is a line disclosed in the field, or that a line enclosed in the field is the field? A field, the line, the melismatic field—

this field,

where the wind "holds its breath," and my throat—and my throat,
a handful of dirt, and my tongue of lilies, and life an incident, a spandrel of the field and the arch-light, the brain and the birch—

but the birch in the brain the shape of the brain, the light in
the brain the brain. The brain in the light, not,—

"Each in each," reads the lark-shook birch from the tongue, "to see the field is not to read it."

"Each in each," reads the gnomon tongue from the foundered field, the—

Gerard Manley Hopkins Drafts the Light

". . . I am writing a popular account of Light and the Ether . . . and my hope is to explain things thoroughly and make the matter, as far as I go in it, perfectly intelligible."

–Hopkins

Empedocles taught fire behind the eye: the eye's diaphanous membrane lets loose those leaves of light which congregate to the perceived body. Plato, to a degree, agrees: fire, fawn-fire, leaps from forests in the deep eye, mingles with sunlight, erects a Body of Vision: a sill, swelling and shriveling, ruled by swivels of its soul, where things touched by light—body, body of a boy, the beauty of him—"enter seer through the eyes." ~~But the eye is a limb of the mind, and the mind is eyes of Christ. Channels to teeming charnel: whiskers on barleystalks and river's skin two million strokes, boys lanky as barleystalks; sea flashing silver, a coiled tiger; boys~~ with striped ~~socks and damp lips, Malebranche in laps under an ash; and a blot on the long ash, and blonde-down burls of thigh, and its rushes, and its moles, and the fruit on the ash, the hitch and plait of the shirt taut in the teeth, the slipped inches of hip, and it's a thrush on the ash when the eye is a hand of flesh and the hand fills the hand fills~~ To Aristotle, light is satiation (Actuality) of a medium desiring (Potentiality) transparency; objects with potentiality to color, when in light, attain actuality to color. Color enters the glassy nave of the eye via air and thence rides blood down to the summing heart, that gatherer-of-senses, the Sensus communis. Vision, says Aristotle, is the soul of the eye, the Final Cause breathing purpose into animal.

~~But the eye is a branch of mind~~ The ancients were wrong: the soul witnesses light, mote among mote, but does not forge it. Light performs out of doors. How, then, the sojourn in the eye? Look—boys dive into the Liffey; they float there, ~~skin~~ The tigery ocean reels the river in and with it a garland of ripening boys. Space intervening upon the eye and burl what it sees is not empty, being infused with such riparian fluid, the Ether, which bears light just as water bears boys to the sea. ~~Vision happens in a kind of estuary: the eye is limb of the~~ The ethereal medium, posits Newton, is far more rarefied than air, more elastic, and upon contact vibrates more minutely: the vibrations of air "made by a man's ordinary voice succeeding at more than half a foot or a foot distance, but those of ether at a less distance than the hundredth-thousandth part of an inch." Ether palpitates, expanding and compressing: when crumbs of light take compressed ether-parts, the denseness brought about by compression Reflects light; when ether expands, light sluices into that interstice between two vibrations (as the drop of the foot through an imagined step), and is Refracted. Vision, then, is a happening in mingles of ether and sparked flesh. In the eye's proscenium, the Retina, is the sheer meshing (like pithwork under an orange rind) of the ends, or Capillamenta, of the Optic Nerve. Light sets these pulsing, and the nerve carries vibration into the sensorium of the brain, which translates movement to color, to vision, vision of the beauty of a boy, vision of the beauty of this vision of a boy.

But ether is so rarefied as to be invisible, and still ether folds light. One sees light but not ether. Where, then, ends ether, where begins light? Put another way: ether is self, say, and light desire. Is desire self? Certainly not, yet each acts upon the other. ~~Lord, why does my desire make me in your eyes?~~ When one is desirous, what is meant is "I am alight in desire, light with desire, heavy with it;" inside all that yearning, self and desire intertwined. Carrying this through, then: ether is a thing forever alight with desire; take light away, and there is no need for ether. Yet, light propagates. So, something shall bear it.

The New Astronomy

The speaker is Katharina Kepler (1546–1622), mother of astronomer Johannes Kepler. In 1615, Katharina was accused of witchcraft and underwent trial with Johannes defending her. She was proven innocent.

This you say is the universe: one flute, two violas, one horn, two cellos

And around the earth, between planets, some force,

An angle, some flesh but the flesh of music, an *x*

Lulling all the worlds into the gentlenesses of cows.

Much talk of magnets. Magnets, water, brooms, light, the light which can be gathered like breath

In lenses, in hands, in mirrors, and *x* may act as light does

Passing through spaces not really present, not being present, having *no* present beingness, *not* being in places, not being *in* places, not being in *places*, not being in places o but *between*, not being *between* places, not *being* between places but, but, still, yes, although, hitherto its wherewithal keeping apart dodecadragons et cetera, and so on, so to speak . . .

I have almost understood you—once—that night was bright

Bright as befits a place with desire in it—and—

And the wind was sharp and full—it weeded and raked

And whistled through the streets far below and the fields

My neck and your face, for anything, to stop it or feed it.

Then, we both looked up—

A quiet fire, a stony fire, a thistle caught ember

When I was asked to confess

Again and again the fire was behind me.

Confess I entered barred houses the calf ridden to death

The skull the sexton the concoctions the bent girl I was

Shown long dull entrails on paper. Forced to read them.

But how could I?

The lord's word will be apparent to those of the lord.

I said from the paper The lord's words will be apparent only to those of the lord.

I was shut in oak.

I smelt my insides.

I was shown each glittering tooth of my executioner all the possibilities of my body

I forced my knees

To my chest my feet

Into corners my eyes

Into knees till I saw a red that was not

Red till I was a place on the earth, one crammed point on the earth.

A place on the earth was named Katharina the wretched

Desire filled Katharina and she became

Heavy the tongue of my grace or my desire

She stammered against the red wall of my desire

The red roof of my grace — my lord

Peel each vein from me —

Find that despite me I have been, been yours, my lord, my lord

Yours all throughout your poured years, your hours

How much I've wept I weep no longer

Among the years how long the hour the life

How long made with what alchemy craft

That only cowed, crushed, I recognize —

Still — but been yours this throat

Yours this heart

My lord with a knife

I cut the meat given. I drink spit.

I add the hours to my voice

To voices of worms nettles burdock hemlock

Cuckoos my aunt stewed up on the stooped bluff

A spruce in the fire swung like a door the wind that yanks its crown is not the wind that plays

In the fields ago —

Away from the Empire — letters come and go slowly and at heavy expense.

Scurrying across the papers the maps only murmur to me, and only in Benedict's hateful spit.

No longer my fields, my nettles, attars, my acids—

No longer my Leonberg.

Here where the sky is the wormy pink of a scraped throat the wind is flying away

Like my voice in search of some anger, my voice flies away

Like the wind looking for a word, away into what is this little that is

Which you say has the sun for the center, a center, the sun borrows from no central fire but is a borrower nonetheless, yes, like everything else, which means that I am *completely* within my rights to write for a telescope, or some lenses at—

Today is far, bright.

I am a blister in a blue mouth.

I go to the fields to suckle an ire.

O between my hands and the vast light

Only dandelions clotting in light raw as milk

The embracing light, the wrinkling light—

In my fields I walked, I plucked

My herbs said the words of my herbs as I pluck hold weigh prove

Dissolve Barwinek Bobownik through the vastness

Between my hands

Through all the places on the earth

The wind flies away — something sung — is that what he meant, you, I mean —

All the hours on the crammed earth —

Oaks bright in the light between them.

A poppy in the sun pants faster —

I count each tree.

One, two, beyond all the way there —

Now I am less afraid, but why of

What light netting the trees

Turning, molding, separating, making each tree, making each shape an *Each*, a *One* —

One Oak. Thick, blotted, — an oak weighs what, how?, four — baffling

Where is my anger?

Where is Katharina?

You might know —

You who have been you

You who have been — who will be my son

Have you understood me?

I wipe my face.

Tonight I will press eyelashes between the pages of your books

Johannes—Johannes!—

You are my son—

You write letters to a man in Italy—

Schubert's Moments Musicaux No. 2

"Light takes the tree . . ."
–Roethke

but at Mud Run and its deep beeches and its cardinals plump
as embroidery and its RV's and its darners and its condoms
like comets in the shrubs it's the tree which not takes take
hinting purpose, the tree which floats into the long O long
slow tree sleepwalks into the low light

near Pittsburgh grand in his birchy bones my appa dandling
his bottles singing Tamil songs older than he so here in Mud
Run I want to build a hovel. Armfuls of plums and honey and
a pile of books for sustenance. Lying on my back my head out
of doors asterism whip-poor-will the open palm of space cupping

earth the nightjar. I hum Schubert I skin a plum far in the alone
I learn the name of each star Algenib Markab Enif Scheat all far
all too far too far to change the spit the spit bright plums the pit
near Mud Run where I cherish this sparrow-footprint gashing
Mud Run's water. Minnow or miracle? The brook the light

the light in the river the dusk. Widening. In the dusk Mud Run
running nowhere deepening.

Fugue

Strange, strangebird, how did you get here? Dawnflush handfuls buckling the neck, and my tongue a pilgrim pulled east—lightplay—pinched pitch plucked past heart to wrist pressed knuckle, one long lake swollen, four cascades, coral, my lips sul ponticello bows a wail—music—music—you, bird, are—that in which music—*music*—broods, burnishes, lashes, lashed here, and here, and here—*here*—this estuary of breaths and gaps—on skin my fingers sweeping: children in the breakers playing upward borne to, past rose in selving—stunned now, *how* back in places once played in—how, *why* did you get here?—straight in the heart of this this thousandbeaked blackness whose breast soughs barren, Cosmos himself a night-bird, strangebird—no song tolls *no*, no song coos, no—nightveiled night-bird, nightshot neverresting nightbird set not to nights, to nights, but night, but night, but night but night and music-yearning and all he is is all he's not. He's not Is—He *is* not Is—is not Is—not Is—no Is—sigh, soot, wide wild wanting wildly veiled sparrow, syrinx, heart-thrush, O Strange! Listen two winds lustdrenched for our flute—*how* did you get here?

Sea Variation

The sea heavy as a trombone.
Deep out of this sea the man yanked
a long silver fish which glared

and shook and shone. Another man reading
the New York Times brought home
his line invisible in the sun.

Bodies in the glare were dark commas on the bench.
In Mosul, said the paper, the garbagemen have again started
work and rake through human remains.

Everything That Is Not the Case

The squat, cream-colored, two-storied house
with the stucco balcony above the gutter
(into which she throws Fanta bottlecaps,
hibiscus buds, strands or clumps of hair
for hours coaxed and unraveled from her white comb's
airy little spaces) (once her father's,
now her husband's), crawls to the edge
of the side mirror, her husband's — but —
                                                            he, this other, has told her something —
and she hasn't yet said anything —
what is there to say, what's there to say — so —
so she quotes a poem she has read that morning — and —
she pretends that he's interested — then that he *could* be interested
in these kinds of things — he's native, after all, as he would say —
books and songs and stories — yes, yes, he's too shy to ask — he needs a teacher —
she, even she, could be the teacher, Sandipani to his Krishna —
he could in turn teach her English — and he could —

A housefly plummets over the glass edge.
A plastic bottle with a crushed mouth
replaces it, already begins to recede
into the silver, neck pointing at
the lost house.
                              Black birds or blackbirds or
nightbirds or birds out in night — or
errant newspapers; all rustle the same way,
and it is vast. The moon hovers at the bottom
or on the surface of the mirror.
                                                    "I don't like
the receptionist," she says, "I don't like
this mot — "
                        No! " — hotel." He takes her hand.
She winces.

"I jammed my thumb," she says. He kisses it.
She lifts a book from her red handbag, flips through.

It is human nature to stand in the middle of a thing,
old toilers, soil makers: O, Roger, Mackerel, Riley!

Soiled toilers, old makers. Toil, toilers,
soilers, tailors — sailors! — Ned, Nellie, Chester;
the car hums a song through her, or she hums
through the car, her bowels are moving, why? —
Because she feels, strange to say, but still, the only
word which says this feeling, not an emerging
but a fore-emerging, a "foreshadowing,"
the shadow of an arriving body
playing in the sands and and a cat on the road,

a tail in the mirror. Three temples.
Five monkeys on a parapet. Film posters:
Naay Baghavan, Nyaya Naay, Nyaya Baghavan.
The Cooum River. The beach, the lighthouse.
The vendors, the perfume in her blouse, the ships
on a meniscus, a kite, the night, the moon a discus.
The peanut carts, the smell of the sea and tomorrow
or the day after, the kite, the carts, the stale-rain smell,
the hot-blouse smell of the sea, and the sea all for the last time,
all for the very last time but now —

Chennai. Now. Now —
now behind them. Now night.
Now soft as petals, dogs' ears, pencildust...

She wakes the second time to the TV, saliva, and sliced apples.
A soap opera in English, the kind her sister
makes fun of, but which she likes, though she
can't follow the too-fast talk. The bedside
window open to a moon black-eyed by

a halo. A horse neighs in the TV—
three gunshots and the sound of sand-on-sand.
Death is, she thinks or is it a dream, is ultimate numbness,
but wasted numbness, numbness unfelt; but numbness
after pain is felten ecstasy.
Once—last week?—he confessed he cries when animals
die on TV. She was repulsed by the confession.
The act, "the principle of it!" as he would say, and his red apple-cool fist—
She imagines his wife in the room now, dabbing his eyes,
kissing his forehead. Is something unfelt still felt
as unfelt? Is there a something, is there a nothing?
He snivels into her white neck.
And, together, they snivel and kiss in ecstasies—
o comfortable grief, o Riley, o Mackerel, o—
                                                            The wife
makes a bird movement and sees *her*
on the bed. The wife is horrorstruck o
the chrysalis drops, revealing a not-full not-flat breast
slightly purple around the nipple. She touches herself before them,
softly, softly, one foot in their kingdom of intimacies,
they stand at the bed's foot bowing, as ashamed as her, and all
three partake in this truth as though sacrament:
she is incapable of being loved. Incapable.
Of being—

His voice somewhere above her. His Little Rock
voice all the way from Arr-ken-saw, USA.
Too-big teeth strip a filament of blood
from too-plump chapped lips. She says,
"Horses are dead?"
                        "Horses?"
                                "TV."
                                        "Dream."
                                                "TV?"
                                                        "Quick Draw McGraw."

• • •

—but the receptionist has a glass eye.
The blue plush dice hanging on the rearview
mirror still says FOUR despite one dot being missing. How?
The road aglow with rain, and dusk undiluting
into night, night diluting into dusk, the hotel—no!—
motel relishing the word, its cheapness—is that pink dot mangled
in the tail of a raindrop. The radio
sings of honeyed Spanish sunsets. She stretches
on her seat watching him without shyness.
Shadowtendrils free themselves from under
thighthicktreetrunks. His forehead is too big
his face is a pink moon which sweats easily.
Unkempt chesthair down and up the V of his
undershirt. Sweatstains under his arms and
he is balding and he *touched* her! The wheel
quakes under his grip. She grabs his right hand
his big red right hand and puts it on her thighs.
He squeezes to bruise, she always forgets he is missing a tooth
until she sees the gap the gap thegapgapgap   ohgapgod living
a gap
                    a gap life life the gap of Gaps   the opposite of
                    an opposite of a word
                              but shy to everyone but him because of this   o how he
                    dissolves her   she is incapable she is incapable of being—

What would you do if I called your wife she says
he is angry or as angry as he can be anyway
she can't mention wives but can her sister who he called gorgeous so she *won't*

                      but he squeezes her through her sourmilk sari

her dirt-in-milk-skin darker than her sister's milk her pretty sister beyond the handbag

                                        but she incapable
of being loved or else her husband would have learned to love
                    ten years of gap of ten years of gap agapeagape like an ear an hour a year
          or ten years

• • •

or
maybe he in his own
silent ineffable uncaring cruel though he has never

beat her her mother said wistfully, stroking her daughter's hair, he never beats you
never lays a hand on her as the English

novels say aloof almost almost God-like way

apparently I don't believe in God can you have
two thoughts
simultaneous

do you switch between
one
and another but so
so imperceptibly ten years

Is the thinker
inthethought her youngyoungyoung sister
or the thought inthethinker

but no hard
to think about or feel about butbutbut anything unfelt is nothing
but nothing but nothing once

her father's now now her husband's now I grow old, I grow old, I shall
wear my sari rolled,
herfathernowherhusbandnowherfathernow thoughtinthethinkeroutinthefieldsofthought

now
black milk of God has never laid a hand on anything

incapable of being
Curving back within myself

• • •

I create again and again and again and again
Trees sway inside a raindrop rolling down the mirror and again.

There here is no escaping being in a world where everything is possible and so
nothing is not possible
a gap is impossible.

Next week? she says though she doesn't think she'll be here
(where?)
"We'll see, beautiful," he says straightening her sari but he winks

what beauty where beauty why beauty in disfiguration in such
hollows of orphanness he *touched* her

sky glutted at the seams flooded gleaming grows deep as a grape in its deepening bruising.

Now, night.

Her underwear is soiled.

Her mother once worried about her.

Her mother was a reader despite her father but her sister abroad is beautiful and a writer.

The monsoon this season is dusty.

Her mother held her and held her and held her.

The car was a Fiat.

There are many countries in which she doesn't exist.

"I write for my mom and sister, not myself. No one else. I don't need to write for anyone else," her sister says in an interview.

• • •

The capital of Andaman is Port Blair.

The capital of Kiribati is Tarawa.

The capital of Neerkavitha is Roslin.

The cloudscuds: pelt, tarred lion-mane.

The cat had made kittens under those stairs. Her father drowned them.

The white cat roams the neighborhood.

The teacup: speckled with two-day-old coffee.

A husband's, the husband's, her husband's mouth was on its rim, where her own mouth has been many times.

Circumference, and the crickets.

The white cat never enters her house. Once her father's.

Betty and Veronica and *Tintin* and *Tinkle Digest* and *Ananda Vikatan* on the wicker table.

On the floor, through the dull blue grates of the verandah—the mesh of oldnight or fawnday. Her handbag is red, and says HERMES, and is from San Bernardino in California in America.

She empties it— *An Anthology of World Poetry*. Keys, coins, rupees, razor, cellphone, napkins, mirror, almonds, browning jasmine, kumkuma, Cadbury's, pencil, mother, sister, nephew, child, Fair & Lovely,—

She gathers herself.

She is gathering herself.

The City Opposite Nineveh

Pier 7, San Francisco

Then came the white sisters clapping to the wave's progress
and that was Emancipation—
jubilation, O jubilation—

vanishing swiftly
as the sea's lace dries in the sun . . .

—Walcott

Variation One

Lovely as milk, smooth as a knell,
bodiless and made of breaths,
a blue bed of pollen,

lace, mesh, the sea ran
like a prayered tongue, the waves
shining where they fell, so many eyes of needles.

Variation Two

Streaks of wet pastel, the sea around the bridge,
smudged on, smudged between delaminated glass,
sounds of one hand clapping, the sea of commas—

sea tarnished beneath the cliff—
marbling, fleecing, breathing
jasmine unravelling in a skittish wind.

Variation Three

The sea was drying its laces
in the sun. The bored wind
nosed one corner of translucent

paper. From the pier, three
lines went down into the brassy
sea which shone in belted buckles.

Variation Four

The sea heavy as a trombone.
Deep out of this sea the man yanked
a long silver fish which glared

and shook and shone. Another man reading
the *New York Times* brought home
his line invisible in the sun.

Bodies in the glare were dark commas on the bench.
In Mosul, said the paper, the garbagemen have again started
work and rake through human remains.

Variation Five

The whipping marbling fleecing sea drove
wind up my nostrils.
My body in the glare was a bead the wind and the light threaded

threaded the wind crept back the mouth of me
the light blew through
the singing gaps of me.

The wind crept back out the mouths
of two of me with the sea
slaughtering between them the light

blew through
the singing gaps
of them.

One buckled but
the other was
singing—

Variation Six

Yet the other was singing, buckling: o
o lovely in milks, in wreathes,
lovely in breaths,

the sea shivers like a prayered tongue—
jubilation, o jubilation,
vanishing swiftly,
as the sea dries its laces in the sun

drying the refuse of faces
faces not there faces no longer there
faces there where the sea was where I was

on a bent green bench
holding and pouring
a singing where I was—

Variation Seven

Where I was was
Mosul.
Where I was
was Mosul by the Tigris
Mosul the Green
Mosul

Mosul the Pearl
Mosul
Mosul the Remaining City

steeped in stink and human remains.
But where an I was
was all the waves.

Variation Eight

Burl of the gnarled green
sea in its milkskins, beneath the bridge
wrinkling like grapeskin.

Where I was, all the waves.
Each falling into the sea.
Each a knock-kneed lamb.

A Lattice

"In the morning they were still singing,
and I was still walking."
—*Mike Good*

The piece below can be read by multiple voices. The leading voice starts anywhere in the piece and can travel up or down the lines. When the first voice reaches its third line or thereabouts, the second voice enters anywhere and reads. Other voices enter and leave alike.

sentential deep water of which grammar, baring which river grammar—what grammar—of what
baring if nothing hid, what waters, what river and, then, now, what river in or by what
water—o what river of which water waters what gates—what gates in which pearls and toads, days
leaping fathoms, of what state, what gate in which something, some, some o four-gated bard river
o going of jeweled mirrors, serac river, what something, which nothing, or none, none at all—
not unremembered, below was invisible, all-involved, at the highest of the high
drawn and bowed and emptied—the tidal voices blooming in themselves, apart, private, furtive—
lit in ornate radium—black array, frog-fat cherries, deep transparent watermelons
experienced of trees dense, dark trees, fluvial, mastering—and the silty viola—
pungent from faraway—jewel sewn to the heart of the blue day—stronger than memory
o Blue Neck all the boles of the dark affluent in trees—on high marrows, the drawn mountain
meandering meanings—and below sealed—and opaque *I cannot experience his voice*—

—and let alone a month let a year alone—the day tonight still the day of the morning's

day, let alone breath—this this measured on a pane or in a frame, or a measure—a thought

same, the same as hung above the lines on day—so the day's thought the day of or in a thought—

a thought's thought of the molt of the day years of thought—if a year's thought a year then a fathom's

thought a fathom—but a thought neither both or—anyway this morning's ergodic day—or

this this's morning's day or in the day of yesternight arose yester's next, blue night—now

morning's day's day but again not either but nor nought—still this—left—this net of let-alones—

of same states *it's-time*'s netted no-net, a rain-net—alone—its thought of nets of the nets of

days and rains alone—lets—a verse-ish-ness a thought of nets—a month or a year or a breath

toiling rain—ponchos skippets debts—debts debts debts of course debts—debts of day, dayslong debts of breath—

river of debts fruitless river, river of bells, beads, gauze river o river of coins

toiling sapphire, ashen-elbowed river, o river of merit which cannot step twice

in yourself, step once, step not at all—of which tether, which water—sun colored glass, dustless

“La route chante . . .”

for Lhasa de Sela

"La route chante . . ." is arranged in a circle of fourths. To make a poem, sound some chords which appeal to you. Then find those same chords in the image on the previous page and match them with the phrase below.

For example, I played the chords on the left below and matched them to their respective phrases to create the poem on the right. A musical setting follows:

C minor	O you poor fool,
F minor	Little descant
G♯ minor	staggering inside:
B♭ minor	Lhasa's eyes,
B♭ major	Lhasa's lips:
G major	jewels, brief jewels.
G♯ minor	Staggering inside,
E♭ minor	you can only end.

"La route chante..."

13

27

41

O you poor fool, o lit-tle des-cant! o – you poor fool, you lit – tle des – cant sta-gger-ing in – si – de

Lha-sa's eyes Lha – sa – 's lips Je – – wels

Brief je – – wels Stag – ger – ing in – side You can you can

can on – – – ly end

Sea Variation

One was singing,
the other buckling—

Notes

1. "**At Road's End—Lincoln City, Oregon**" was inspired by medieval motets, choral pieces where different texts are sung simultaneously. The third voice of the poem is reading Emily Dickinson.
2. The word "patti" in "**A Poem**" is the Tamil word for "grandmother."
3. The title "**Fear was my father . . .**" is taken from Theodore Rotheke's poem "The Lost Son."
4. "**The Age of Waters**" is indebted to the polyphonic work of Robert Bringhurst, particularly *The Blue Roofs of Japan*. The sections of the poem can be read in any order. "The Age of Waters" also quotes, cites, or paraphrases:
   - Chris Anderson, *Edge Effects: Notes From an Oregon Forest* (University of Iowa Press, 1993), x-xi.
   - Ellen Morris Bishop, *In Search of Ancient Oregon: A Geological and Natural History* (Timber, 2010).
   - Sandra H.B. Clark, *Birth of the Mountains: The Geologic Story of the Southern Appalachian Mountains* (USGS, 2001).
   - Frank N. Egerton, "A History of the Ecological Sciences, Part 27: Naturalists Explore Russia and the North Pacific During the 1700s," *Bulletin 89* no. 1 (2008): 39-60.
   - Farmer, Judith A., and Kenneth L. Holmes. *An Historical Atlas of Early Oregon* (Historical Cartographic Publications, 1973).
   - George Herbert, *Herbert: Poems* (Everyman's Library, 2004), 206.
   - Gerard Manley Hopkins, *Gerard Manley Hopkins: The Major Works* (OUP Oxford, 2009).
   - Dell Hymes, "In Vain I Tried to Tell You," University of Pennsylvania Press eBooks, 1981, https://doi.org/10.9783/9781512802917.
   - Dell H. Hymes, *Now I Know Only so Far: Essays in Ethnopoetics* (U of Nebraska Press, 2003).
   - Melville Jacobs, *Kalapuya Texts* (U of Washington Press, 1945), 91.
   - Louis Kenoyer, *My Life: Reminiscences of a Grand Ronde Reservation Childhood* (OSU Press, 2017).
   - Marianne Moore, *The Poems of Marianne Moore* (Penguin, 2005), 136.

- Jarold Ramsey, *Reading the Fire: The Traditional Indian Literatures of America* (U of Washington Press, 1999).
- "The diary of Philip C. Van Buskirk," The Philip C. Van Buskirk Archive, September 30, 2017, https://vanbuskirk.commons.gc.cuny.edu/.
- "Steller's Journal of the Sea Voyage from Kamchatka to America and Return on the Second Expedition, 1741-1742," Wisconsin Historical Society American Journeys, 2003, https://content.wisconsinhistory.org/digital/collection/aj/id/5999.
- Travis Williams, *The Willamette River Field Guide* (Timber Press, 2009).
- Henry Zenk, "Notes on Native American Place-Names of the Willamette Valley Region," Oregon Historical Quarterly 109, no. 1 (January 1, 2008): 6–33, https://doi.org/10.1353/ohq.2008.0092.

5. "**Schubert's Piano Sonata in B-flat**" quotes from the song "Warm Blood" by Carly Rae Jepsen.
6. The title "**My peace is gone, my heart is heavy . . .**" is taken from the first lines of "Gretchen am Spinnrade," originally written by Goethe.
7. "**Re: re: No Gimmick . . .**" was inspired by spam emails. The Prince's sonnet is a paraphrase of Britney Spears's ". . . Baby One More Time."
8. The line "letters come and go slowly and at heavy expense" in "**The New Astronomy**" is taken from a letter written by Johannes Kepler and quoted in Arthur Koestler's *The Sleepwalkers: A History of Man's Changing Vision of the Universe* (Penguin, 1968).
9. **The City Opposite Nineveh** uses a stanza from Derek Walcott's poem "The Sea is History" as its theme.
10. The title "**La route chante . . .**" is taken from the song "La marée haute" by Lhasa de Sela. The piece also quotes from J.P. Seaton's translation of Yuan Mei, an Emily Dickinson Letter, and the song "Desdeñosa" by Lhasa de Sela.
11. **Recordings** of these poems are freely available on Varun Ravindran's website: www.varunravindran.com/recordings

Acknowledgments

Thank you to the following journals and magazines for publishing poems appearing in this collection:

The Adroit Journal, Pleiades, Notre Dame Review, FOLIO, cream city review, West Branch, Tinderbox Poetry, Prelude, Radar Poetry, Kenyon Review Online, Denver Quarterly, Massachusetts Review, Prolit, GUESTHOUSE, mercury firs, Dreginald, Apartment Poetry

Several poems also appeared in the chapbook *Intermezzi* from Almost Perfect Press.

Love and a play bow to Coyote.

Love to Baobab Press: Christine E. Kelly, Laura Wetherington, Danilo John Thomas.

Love for the kind words: Samiya Bashir, Su Cho, Jane Huffman, Michael Joseph Walsh, and Michael Zapruder

Love to the friends, teachers: Mike Good, Emily Maust, Inga Schmidt, Frank Karioris, William Repass, Karla Lamb, Clare Welsh, Christy Owens, Catherine Gammon, Brent Nakamoto, George Ellis, Jill Pearlman, Patrick Walsh, Jan Ravindran, Surya Ravindran, Chandra Kannan, Ava Cipri, Julie Gatti, Mohini Wagle-Schmitt, Benjamin Binder and the Neighborhood Zen Sangha.

Love to Patrick Walsh, Jan Ravindran, Surya Ravindran, Chandra Kannan, Mike Good.

Love, deep bows to Catherine Gammon.

Love to Patrick Walsh.

May whatever merit attained through these words be dedicated to the liberation of all beings.

Photo Credit: Clare Welsh,
clarewelsh.format.com

Varun Ravindran was born in Chennai, India, and lives in Pittsburgh, Pennsylvania. He graduated from Duquesne University. His work has appeared in various literary journals like *Kenyon Review Online*, *Denver Quarterly*, and *mercury firs*.

The body text of *Betweenness* is set in Constantia, a modulated wedge-serif typeface designed by John Hudson primarily for continuous text in both electronic and paper publishing.

The headers are set in **Essonnes**. Designed in 2011 by Hames Hultquist-Todd, and born of a union between Didot experimentation, late Victorian extravagance, and contemporary pragmatism, Essonnes is a type system which brings both the familiarity and creativity of a Didone together with the situational requirements of the 21st century.